make

star quilts

11 Stellar Projects to Sew

C&T PUBLISHING

Text, photography, and artwork copyright © 2016 by C&T Publishing, Inc.

Publisher: Amy Marson

Creative Director: Gailen Runge

Editors: Alice Mace Nakanishi and Joanna Burgarino

Cover/Book Designer: April Mostek

Production Coordinator: Zinnia Heinzmann

Photography by Diane Pedersen, Christina Carty-Francis, and Nissa Brehmer, of C&T Publishing, unless otherwise noted

For further information and similar projects, see the book listed after each artist's bio.

Published by C&T Publishing, Inc., P.O. Box 1456, Lafayette, CA 94549

Printed in China

10 9 8 7 6 5 4 3 2 1

Contents

11 STAR QUILTS

Night Skies

Beth Ferrier

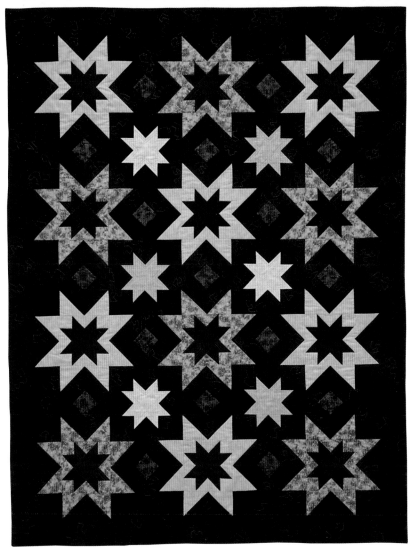

Large, simple blocks—put together using some of the best sneaky piecing tricks around—make this quilt an easy weekend project. Make it for one of the superstars in your life.

Designed, pieced, and quilted by Beth Ferrier

BETH FERRIER is an accomplished quilter who describes her style as "rebellious traditional." She is forever in search of easy and simply elegant solutions to quilting challenges. Everything she designs is geared toward teaching skill-expanding tips and techniques. Beth lives in Green Bay, Wisconsin.

WEBSITE: applewoodfarmquilts.com

This project originally appeared in *Sneaky Piecing* by Beth Ferrier, available from C&T Publishing.

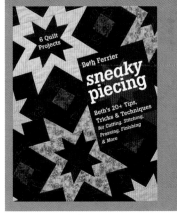

Materials

Yardage is based on 40"-wide fabric unless otherwise noted. Yardage amounts have been rounded up to include a little wiggle room.

BACKGROUND FABRIC: 4 yards* for pieced blocks

DARK RED FABRIC: 1 yard for pieced blocks and binding

BRIGHT BLUE FABRIC: 1/3 yard for pieced blocks

LEMON YELLOW FABRIC: 1/3 yard for pieced blocks

YELLOW FABRIC: 7/8 yard for pieced blocks

DARK YELLOW FABRIC: 1/3 yard for pieced blocks

ORANGE FABRIC: 7/8 yard for pieced blocks

BACKING FABRIC AND BATTING: Sized for quilt

ZIP-TOP BAGS: 7 gallon size, labeled 1–7

ROTARY CUTTER, MAT, AND RULER (a 12½" square ruler is handy)

TEMPLATE PLASTIC: 3³/8" square (Place in Bag 3.)

* Requires 41" usable fabric width.

Cutting

WOF = width of fabric

As you cut, you'll organize your cut pieces into bags as indicated.

BACKGROUND FABRIC

Cut 3 strips 9¼" × WOF. Subcut:

  12 squares 9¼" × 9¼". *Place in Bag 1.*

Cut 13 strips 4½" × WOF. Subcut:

  4 segments 4½" × 40½".
  Place in Bag 7.

From each of 2 remaining strips, subcut:

  1 segment 4½" × 36½". *Place in Bag 7.*

  1 square 4½" × 4½". *Place in Bag 5.*

From each of 2 remaining strips, subcut:

  1 segment 4½" × 24½". *Place in Bag 7.*

  3 squares 4½" × 4½". *Place in Bag 5.*

From the 5 remaining strips, subcut:

  40 squares 4½" × 4½". *Place in Bag 5.*

Cut 5 strips 6½" × WOF. Subcut:

  34 rectangles 6½" × 4½".
  Place 24 in Bag 6 and 10 in Bag 7.

Cut 6 strips 2⅞" × WOF. Subcut:

  70 squares 2⅞" × 2⅞".
  Place 46 in Bag 3 and 24 in Bag 2.

DARK RED FABRIC

Cut 1 strip 4½" × WOF. Subcut:

  6 squares 4½" × 4½". *Place in Bag 4.*

  4 squares 2⅞" × 2⅞". Mark the diagonal on the wrong side.
  Place in Bag 2.

Cut 1 strip 3⅜" × WOF. Subcut:

  6 squares 3⅜" × 3⅜". *Place in Bag 3.*

Cut 2 strips 2⅞" × WOF. Subcut:

  20 squares 2⅞" × 2⅞". Mark the diagonal on the wrong side.
  Place in Bag 2.

Cut 8 strips 2" × WOF for the binding.
Place in Bag 7.

LEMON YELLOW FABRIC

Cut 1 strip 4½" × WOF. Subcut:

  3 squares 4½" × 4½". *Place in Bag 7.*

  10 squares 2½" × 2½". Mark the diagonal on the wrong side.
  Place in Bag 6.

Cut 1 strip 2½" × WOF. Subcut:

  14 squares 2½" × 2½". Mark the diagonal on the wrong side.
  Place in Bag 6.

BRIGHT BLUE FABRIC

Cut 2 strips 3⅜" × WOF. Subcut:

  17 squares 3⅜" × 3⅜". *Place in Bag 3.*

YELLOW FABRIC

Cut 3 strips 4⅞" × WOF. Subcut:

  24 squares 4⅞" × 4⅞". Mark the diagonal on the wrong side.
  Place in Bag 1.

Cut 1 strip 5¼" × WOF. Subcut:

  6 squares 5¼" × 5¼". *Place in Bag 2.*

Cut 2 strips 2½" × WOF. Subcut:

  24 squares 2½" × 2½". *Place in Bag 4.*

DARK YELLOW FABRIC

Cut 1 strip 4½" × WOF. Subcut:

  3 squares 4½" × 4½". *Place in Bag 7.*

  10 squares 2½" × 2½". Mark the diagonal on the wrong side.
  Place in Bag 6.

Cut 1 strip 2½" × WOF. Subcut:

  14 squares 2½" × 2½". Mark the diagonal on the wrong side.
  Place in Bag 6.

ORANGE FABRIC

Cut 3 strips 4⅞" × WOF. Subcut:

  24 squares 4⅞" × 4⅞". Mark the diagonal on the wrong side.
  Place in Bag 1.

Cut 1 strip 5¼" × WOF. Subcut:

  6 squares 5¼" × 5¼". *Place in Bag 2.*

Cut 2 strips 2½" × WOF. Subcut:

  24 squares 2½" × 2½". *Place in Bag 4.*

Construction

Unless otherwise noted, all seam allowances are ¼", and pieces are sewn right sides together. Seams are always pressed away from the background fabric (AFTB).

BIG GEESE UNITS

Using the Five-Square Geese Method (next page) and the pieces in Bag 1, make 24 orange/background and 24 yellow/background Flying Geese units. These should measure 4½" × 8½". *Place in Bag 5.*

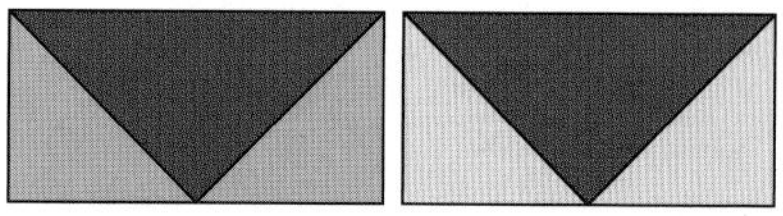

Make 24 of each.

SMALL GEESE UNITS

1. Using the Five-Square Geese Method (next page) and the pieces in Bag 2, make 24 background/orange Flying Geese. These units should measure 2½" × 4½".

2. Repeat Step 1 to make 24 dark red / yellow Flying Geese. Press the seams toward the dark red fabric. *Place the Step 1 and Step 2 units in Bag 4.*

SQUARE-IN-A-SQUARE BLOCKS

1. Using the Square-in-a-Square Method (next page) and the Bag 3 pieces, make 17 bright blue / background Square-in-a-Square blocks. These should measure 4½" × 4½". *Place in Bag 7.*

2. Make 6 dark red / background Square-in-a-Square blocks using the Bag 3 pieces. *Place in Bag 4.*

Five-Square Geese Method

Each goose is made up of 2 small triangles and a large triangle. The small triangles are half-squares; the larger one is a quarter-square. By changing the position of the background fabric, we can have either Flying Geese blocks (with the background fabric as the small triangles) or star points (with the background as the large triangle).

1. Position 2 small squares on opposite corners of the large square, right sides together, so that the lines drawn on the wrong sides connect. Yep, it's okay that the points overlap.

2. Stitch a seam ¼" on each side of the diagonal line. Cut on the line and press the seams away from the background fabric. You now have 2 funny-shaped hearts.

Place small squares in opposing corners, stitch, and cut apart.

3. Place one of the remaining small squares on each of the heart shapes, positioned so that the drawn line splits the cleavage of the heart.

4. Sew a seam ¼" from each side of the line. Cut along the line and press the seam allowances away from the background fabric. Voilà! You have 4 Flying Geese! How sneaky is that?

Stitch on the diagonal across the square, cut apart, and press.

Square-in-a-Square Method

1. Fold the center square in half to make a rectangle, giving it a good crease. Lay it on the stack of triangles so that the fold touches the point at the top and the short side is even with the bottom.

2. Carefully flop the square open; it will be centered on the triangles. See those darned dog ears sticking out on either side of the square? Chop 'em off! You now have 4 triangles, perfectly trimmed to fit the center square, making this block a snap to sew. Cool beans!

Center the folded square over the triangles, unfold, and then cut off the dog-ears.

SMALL STAR BLOCKS

1. Use the small yellow squares, the dark red / yellow Flying Geese, and the dark red squares in Bag 4 to create 6 small star blocks. Arrange the pieces as shown, making sure that each part is turned properly, and then stack the remaining parts on top.

2. Assembly-line sew the left vertical seams. Press the seams toward the dark red fabric.

3. Assembly-line sew the right vertical seams. Press toward the dark red.

4. Sew the cross seams. Press. These 6 blocks should measure 8½″ × 8½″. *Place in Bag 5.*

5. Repeat Steps 1–4 to make 6 blocks with the small orange squares, background/orange Flying Geese, and dark red Square-in-a-Square blocks from Bag 4. Press toward the orange. *Place the 6 blocks in Bag 5.*

BIG STAR BLOCKS

Using the Bag 5 pieces and following the same steps as Small Star Blocks (above), make 6 *each* of orange stars and yellow stars. These blocks should measure 16½″ × 16½″. Set them aside for now. You're nearly done!

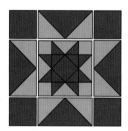 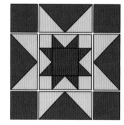

Big star assembly—make 6 of each.

CONNECTING CORNERS

1. Take the 24 lemon yellow 2½″ × 2½″ squares and 12 of the background 6½″ × 4½″ rectangles from Bag 6. Align a lemon yellow square on a corner of the background rectangle so the drawn line cuts across the corner. Sew on the line. Trim away the excess corner fabric and press the seam toward the lemon yellow triangle. Repeat with the 11 remaining background rectangles.

Sew the corners, trim, and press.

2. Place a lemon yellow square on the corner next to the one you just sewed. Repeat Step 1, sewing on the line, trimming, and pressing. *Place in Bag 7.*

Add a second connecting corner. Make 12.

3. Repeat Steps 1 and 2 with the 24 dark yellow 2½″ × 2½″ squares and the remaining 12 background 6½″ × 4½″ rectangles. *Place the finished units in Bag 7.*

Make 12.

SASHING

You're coasting down to the big finish, but first it's time to put together the sashing strips using the pieces in Bag 7. You have three different color placements.

1. Join a dark yellow / background rectangle, a bright blue Square-in-a-Square, and a plain background rectangle end to end, as shown. Make 5.

Sew together end to end. Make 5.

2. Repeat Step 1 with the lemon yellow / background rectangles. Make 5 of these.

Repeat with the lemon yellow pieced units. Make 5.

3. Repeat Step 1 once more with the lemon yellow / background rectangles, bright blue Square-in-a-Square units, and dark yellow / background rectangles. Make 7.

Make 7.

4. Because the pieced sashing rectangles have so many different color placements, it's safest to lay out all the blocks and sashing rectangles to make sure everything is in the correct position. Sewing and pressing the blocks one at a time will eliminate confusion.

Lay out the blocks and sashing.

Quilt assembly

5. Add the sashing and cornerstones from Bag 7 to the blocks.

6. Sew a 4½″ × 36½″ background fabric segment to a 4½″ × 40½″ background fabric segment. Press the seam. Make 2. These are the side borders.

7. Sew a 4½″ × 24½″ background fabric segment to a 4½″ × 40½″ background fabric segment. Press the seam. Make 2. These are the top and bottom borders.

8. Sew the side borders in place and press the seams toward the border. Then sew on the top and bottom borders.

FINISHING THE QUILT
Layer, quilt, block, and bind your quilt.

Seeing Stars

Alex Anderson

FINISHED QUILT: 48½" × 54½"

FINISHED BLOCK: 6" × 6"

TOTAL NUMBER OF STAR BLOCKS: 27

I love Star quilts, so I guess it's no surprise that I would include one in this book. I decided to emphasize the star motif by making the star points darker than the star centers (or "bellies") and—taking my cue from modern quilters—chose a fresh, sparkling white for the background. As a finishing touch, I dropped in a few random polka dot squares for visual interest and to complement the polka dots I used in some of the blocks.

Designed and pieced by Alex Anderson; machine quilted by Dianne Schweickert

Materials

Fabric amounts are based on a 42" fabric width.

ASSORTED LIGHT TO DARK COLORFUL PRINTS: 1 yard total for stars

WHITE SOLID: 3 yards for block backgrounds, filler strips, filler squares, outer border, and binding

LIGHT PRINT: ¼ yard for filler squares

A TEAL AND A BLUE SUBTLE PRINT: ⅛ yard of each for flat piping

BACKING: 3 yards of fabric (horizontal seam)

BATTING: 53" × 59"

Cutting

All measurements include ¼"-wide seam allowance. Cut strips on the crosswise grain of the fabric (selvage to selvage) unless otherwise noted. See the introduction to Piecing the Blocks (next page) for the number and combination of pieces you'll use for each block.

ASSORTED COLORFUL PRINTS
Cut 108 squares 2⅜" × 2⅜" in matching sets of 4 for star points.

Cut 27 squares 3½" × 3½" for star centers.

WHITE SOLID—*LENGTHWISE GRAIN*
Cut 2 strips 3½" × 42½".

Cut 2 strips 3½" × 54½".

REMAINING WHITE SOLID
Cut 27 squares 4¼" × 4¼" for star-point units.

Cut 108 squares 2" × 2" for block corners.

Cut 11 squares 6½" × 6½" for large filler squares.

Cut 20 rectangles 3½" × 6½" for filler strips.

Cut 4 rectangles 3½" × 12½" for filler strips.

Cut 1 rectangle 3½" × 9½" for filler strip.

Cut 4 squares 3½" × 3½" for small filler squares.

Cut 6 strips 2⅛" × the fabric width for binding.

LIGHT PRINT
Cut 9 squares 3½" × 3½" for filler squares.

BLUE AND TEAL PRINTS—*FROM EACH*
Cut 3 strips 1" × the fabric width.

Construction

PIECING THE BLOCKS

For each of these blocks, use 4 matching 2³⁄₈″ × 2³⁄₈″ squares for the star points, a square 3½″ × 3½″ cut from a different print for the star center, and a square 4¼″ × 4¼″ and 4 squares 2″ × 2″ cut from the white solid for the background.

1. Use 4 matching print squares 2³⁄₈″ × 2³⁄₈″ and a white square 4¼″ × 4¼″ to make 4 Flying Geese units.

Make 4 Flying Geese units.

2. Arrange the 4 units from Step 1, an assorted print 3½″ × 3½″ square, and 4 white 2″ × 2″ squares as shown. Sew the units and squares together into rows; press. Sew the rows together; press.

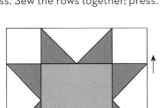

Sew units and squares together into rows.

3. Repeat Steps 1 and 2 to make a total of 27 Star blocks.

ALEX ANDERSON is a founding partner, executive producer, and co-host of the web TV's *The Quilt Show* with Ricky Tims, as well as founding partner of *The Quilt Life* magazine. She has authored 30 books that have sold a combined total of nearly one million copies. Alex lives in Northern California.

WEBSITE: alexandersonquilts.com

This project originally appeared in *Scrap Quilting with Alex Anderson* by Alex Anderson, available from C&T Publishing.

QUILT ASSEMBLY

1. Arrange the blocks, the large and small filler squares, and the filler strips as shown in the quilt assembly diagram.

2. Sew the blocks, squares, and strips together in "neighborhoods" as shown; press.

3. Sew the neighborhoods together; press so that seams fall in opposite directions whenever possible.

4. Sew the 3½″ × 42½″ white outer-border strips to the top and bottom of the quilt. Press the seams toward the border. Sew the 3½″ × 54½″ white outer-border strips to the sides of the quilt; press.

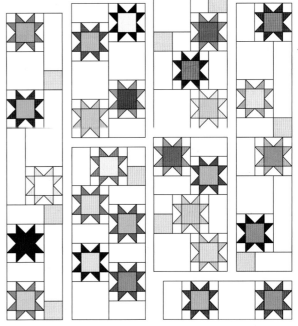

Quilt assembly

FINISHING

1. Layer and baste the quilt, and then quilt as desired. Dianne machine quilted an overall motif of large bubbles and swirls over the entire quilt, picking up on the circles in the many polka dot fabrics.

2. Sew the 1"-wide blue and teal strips together end to end with diagonal seams, and press the seams open. Fold the strip in half, wrong sides together, and press.

3. Trim the batting and backing even with the raw edges of the quilt top. Measure the quilt through the center from top to bottom and from side to side. Cut 2 strips to each measurement from the folded blue/teal strip. With right sides together and raw edges aligned, use a machine basting stitch and a scant ¼" seam to sew the piping strips to the sides, top, and bottom of the quilt.

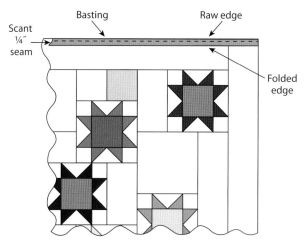

Add piping.

4. Sew the 2⅛"-wide white binding strips together end to end with diagonal seams, and use them to bind the edges of the quilt.

Rum Raisin

Mary Fons

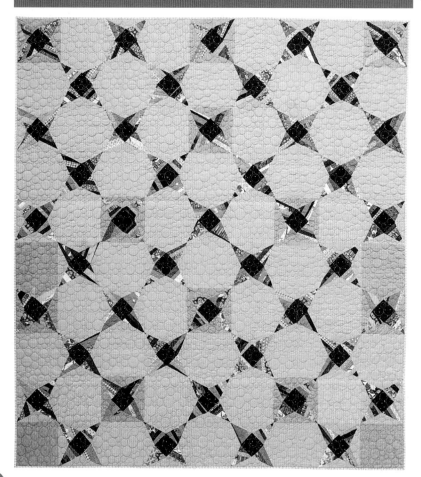

FINISHED QUILT: 90" × 100"

FINISHED BLOCK: 10" × 10"

This quilt is a classic Rocky Road to Kansas pattern. Whenever I see a Rocky Road quilt, naturally I think of ice cream, but I prefer Rum Raisin.

It can be lonely, loving Rum Raisin. It's not a crowd pleaser like cookie dough or vanilla. But the unusual ice cream has an intriguing, sophisticated personality (kind of like pistachio, but with booze).

In homage to all my Rum Raisiennes, this quilt uses up loner scraps. I curated them only as far as deciding that the string-pieced portions would be in warm reds and oranges. I added a few pale shades to let it all breathe and black starry centers to tack it down. The Wedgwood blue behind the stars lets the orphan scraps shine.

Made by Mary Fons; quilted by Sally Evanshank

Materials

Blocks

SCRAPS: approximately 4½ yards total dark reds, dark oranges, and medium oranges; a small amount of pale yellow and/or pale orange; plus a few black scraps tossed in for good measure

WEDGWOOD BLUE SOLID: 9⅝ yards (or variety of solid blues)

DOTTED BLACK: 1⅛ yards

Other supplies

BACKING: 8½ yards total scraps or yardage

BINDING: ⅞ yard of white/black print

BATTING: 98″ × 108″

PAPER PIECING: Foundation paper (You can use typing paper, specialty foundation piecing paper—such as Carol Doak's Foundation Paper, by C&T Publishing—or even newsprint, but be careful using any paper with ink that might rub off.)

FABRIC GLUESTICK

SPECIAL TOOL: Fons & Porter Half and Quarter Ruler (optional)

Cutting

SCRAPS

Cut a lot of strips. Try to cut strips no less than 1½″ wide; smaller than that and they become too narrow for piecing. Anything wider than 3″ is getting too thick; you want each star point to have plenty of variety.

WEDGWOOD BLUE

Cut 30 strips 7″ × width of fabric; subcut into 360 rectangles 3½″ × 7″.

Cut 45 squares 10½″ × 10½″ for setting squares.

DOTTED BLACK

If using optional ruler, cut 10 strips 3½″ × width of fabric; subcut into 180 half-square triangles. *Otherwise,* cut 9 strips 4″ × width of fabric; subcut into 90 squares 4″ × 4″ and cut each square in half diagonally to yield 180 half-square triangles.

BINDING

Cut 10 strips 2½″ × width of fabric.

* Fons & Porter Half and Quarter Ruler

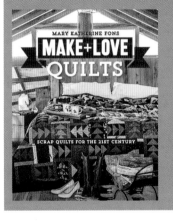
Construction

Seam allowances are ¼″.

STAR BLOCKS

1. Copy the foundation-piecing pattern (page 37) onto foundation paper. Make 180 copies.

2. Join string scraps to create panels that are roughly 8″ × 20″. Make 26 panels.

String panel; make 26.

tip Strips from fat quarters will work just fine in the 8″ × 20″ panels.

3. Cut 180 triangular chunks from the panels (7 from each panel). These don't have to be precise, just large enough to cover the triangle on the foundation paper. Cut at different angles for more variety in the chunks and to get the most from each panel.

Cut chunks to cover triangle.

tip Think of it this way: the lines are on the *back* of the paper. They are what you will be looking at as you sew. It could be said that with paper piecing, you are building a block from the back.

4. Swipe a bit of glue on the front of the paper in Section 1. Place a chunk of string piecing that you cut in Step 2 so it completely covers Section 1.

Place string piecing on Section 1.

5. Place a Wedgwood blue rectangle so it will cover Section 2. Then flip over the blue rectangle so it is right sides together with the string piecing. The Section 2 rectangle needs to be placed so that there will be about a ¼" seam allowance hanging over the sewing line.

Place blue rectangle to cover Section 2.

Flip over blue fabric so it is right sides together with string piecing.

tips To make sure each piece of fabric will cover the appropriate section, pin along the sewing line before sewing and flip the fabric over to make sure the section is covered and there are adequate seam allowances.

● Shorten the stitch length to about 2.0. Using a shorter stitch will make it easier when you tear off the paper after the stitching is done.

6. Use a pin to hold the pieces in place. Flip over the fabric and paper and sew on the line between Section 1 and Section 2.

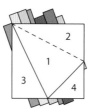

Sew.

7. Press back the blue rectangle. The piece should completely cover the Section 2 triangle on the foundation paper. If it doesn't, rip out the seam and try again. You'll get the hang of it—promise! Once the piece is sewn properly, fold back paper at the seam and trim the seam allowance to ¼".

Press back blue rectangle.

8. Continue sewing on the paper. Add the second blue rectangle and then the black center.

Add second blue rectangle.

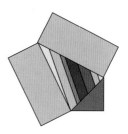

Add black center.

tip You may want to do the string piecing on paper, too. It's not necessary, but some piecers like the stability paper gives them when handling all those long, loose scraps.

....

9. When all the blocks are sewn, use the lines on the paper to trim them with a rotary cutter and ruler to 5½" × 5½" square. Ta-da! You've got a quadrant.

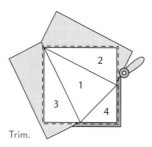

Trim.

Completed quadrant

10. Join 4 block quadrants to complete 1 block. Press the seams in alternate directions so the seams nest when the quadrants are sewn together. Make 45 blocks.

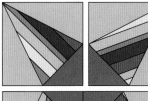

Make 45.

QUILT ASSEMBLY

Take a look at the quilt photo (page 10) and the quilt assembly diagram (above right).

Sew together the blocks into rows, alternating the Star blocks with the setting blocks. Press the seams in alternate directions so they nest when the rows are sewn together. Sew together the rows.

FINISHING

1. Sew together yardage or scraps as needed to make the backing 4"–10" bigger on all sides than the quilt top.

2. Layer the backing, batting, and quilt top. Baste and quilt as you please.

3. Create French fold binding in white/black fabric. Sew the binding to the quilt.

4. Obtain ice cream. Go back to bed.

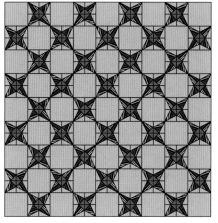

Quilt assembly

B-SIDE

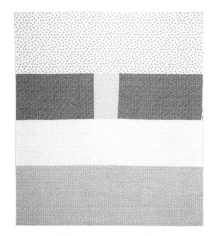

My second favorite ice cream flavor is pistachio. So green had to make an appearance.

Quilt Charm

QUILTING MEMO: Bubbles, bubbles everywhere. Or plump raisins? Either way, it's sweet.

Rainbow II

Jan Krentz

FINISHED QUILT: 66″ × 66″

FINISHED BLOCK: 58″ × 58″

This Broken Star design features split diamonds in a collection of sixteen different fabrics—a medium and darker value fabric for each diamond. The crisp white background fabric provides a place to highlight fabulous quilting, either by hand or machine.

Made by Jan Krentz; quilted by Janet Sturdevant Stuart

JAN KRENTZ is an award-winning, internationally-recognized quilt instructor and designer. Jan's motivating presentations and workshops are packed with practical tips, techniques, and methods to ensure success. She is the author of several C&T books, a DVD, and the fast2cut rulers. Jan lives in Poway, California.

WEBSITE: jankrentz.com

This project originally appeared in *Quick Star Quilts & Beyond* by Jan P. Krentz, available from C&T Publishing.

Construction

1. Sew the 4¼″ strips together in pairs to create 8 strip sets, each with a medium and darker value of the same color. Press seams *open.*

2. Using the 2 parts of the 6½″ diamond pattern (pages 38 and 39) connected together, make a template and cut 2 diamonds from each strip set.

3. Remove the remainder of the stitching, and sew the remaining straight edges of each pair of fabrics.

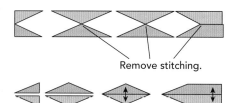

Remove stitching.

Materials and Cutting

Yardage	For	Cutting
2½ yards white	Background	Cut 20 squares 9″ × 9″.
		Cut 2 squares, 13¼″ × 13¼″; cut diagonally twice to yield 8 triangles.
	Border 1	Cut 7 border strips 2″ × 42″ (selvage to selvage).
¼ yard each of the following*: Medium yellow print (1) Darker yellow-orange print (2) Medium green print (3) Darker green print (4) Medium aqua print (5) Darker aqua print (6) Medium blue print (7) Darker blue print (8) Medium purple print (9) Darker purple print (10) Medium orchid purple (11) Darker red-violet print (12) Medium fuchsia pink (13) Darker fuchsia pink (14) Medium red print (15) Darker red print (16)	Split diamonds	Cut 1 strip 4¼″ × 42″ (selvage to selvage) of each.
⅞ yard multicolor stripe	Border 2	Cut 8 border strips 3″ × 42″ (selvage to selvage, perpendicular to the stripe).
⅝ yard fabric	Binding	Cut 2¾″ strips to total 276″ (straight grain or bias).
4¼ yards fabric	Backing	
Batting, 74″ × 74″		

Numbers in parentheses refer to fabric placement in the quilt diagram with color placement (below right).

4. Cut 2 additional diamonds from the fabric combinations for a total of 32 (4 of each color combination).

5. Sew the Broken Star block, referring to the quilt assembly diagram. Press open between diamonds and between squares. Press the other seams toward the squares and triangles.

Quilt assembly.
Red dots indicate set-in seams.

6. Sew the 7 white border strips together end to end. Cut into 4 strips, 66″ long. Sew the multicolor stripe strips into pairs and cut to make 4 strips 72″ long.

7. Sew the borders to the quilt top. Press. (The borders in the photographed quilt are sewn together in strips and then attached with mitered corners.)

8. Layer and baste the quilt top with batting and backing. Quilt as desired and bind.

Quilt diagram with color placement

Lemon Blueberry Pound Cake

Sandy Bonsib

Lemon Blueberry Pound Cake *combines two complementary colors, yellow-orange and blue-violet. Very colorful, this quilt has an unusual circular block and circular setting.*

Made by Sandy Bonsib; quilted by Carrie Peterson

Materials

BLUE-VIOLET FABRICS (15):

13 different, ½ yard each

1 different, ⅓ yard

1 different, ¼ yard

YELLOW-ORANGE FABRICS (21):

13 different, ½ yard each

8 different, ⅓ yard each

BACKING FABRIC:

8 yards (2 horizontal seams)

BINDING FABRIC: ¾ yard

BATTING: 86" × 102"

Cutting

BLUE-VIOLET FABRICS (15)
From each of 13 blue-violet fabrics:

Cut 1 square 4½" × 4½" for a total of 13 squares.

Cut 3 strips 2½" × 42". *From these strips:*

Subcut 8 rectangles 2½" × 6½" for a total of 104 rectangles.

Subcut 8 rectangles 2½" × 4½" for a total of 104 rectangles.

Subcut 8 squares 2½" × 2½" for a total of 104 squares; then draw a diagonal line on wrong side of each square.

 Draw a diagonal line on each blue-violet 2½" × 2½" square.

HINT: Blue-violet, sometimes called *periwinkle*, can be a challenging color to choose. Be careful not to choose fabrics that are too blue or too purple. I start choosing blue-violet by looking at both the blues and the purples (violets) in the fabric store. If there are fabrics in with the blues that look purple or fabrics in with the purples that look blue, they are probably periwinkle.

Likewise, yellow-orange can be a challenging color to choose. If there is a fabric in with the oranges that looks yellow or if there is a fabric in with the yellows that looks orange, these fabrics are probably yellow-orange.

Having said this, try to enjoy the process of choosing your fabrics. This quilt will work even if some fabrics are a little too yellow, too orange, too blue, or too purple. These will add variety and interest to your quilt.

From 1 different blue-violet fabric:
Cut 2 strips 4½" × 42"; subcut
16 squares 4½" × 4½".

From 1 different blue-violet fabric:
Cut 1 strip 4½" × 42"; subcut
8 squares 4½" × 4½".

YELLOW-ORANGE FABRICS (21)
From each of 13 yellow-orange fabrics:
Cut 4 strips 2½" × 42". _From these
strips:_

    Subcut 4 rectangles 2½" × 4½"
    for a total of 52 rectangles.

    Subcut 44 squares 2½" × 2½"
    for a total of 572 squares; then
    draw a diagonal line on wrong
    side of _just 32 squares_ from
    each fabric.

 Draw a diagonal line on
32 yellow-orange
2½" × 2½" squares
from each fabric.

Cut 1 strip 4½" × 42".

    Subcut 2 squares 4½" × 4½"
    for a total of 117 squares.

From each of 8 yellow-orange fabrics:
Cut 2 strips 4½" × 42". _From these
strips:_

    Subcut a total of 11 squares
    4½" × 4½" from each fabric
    for a total of 88 squares.

Construction

_Make sure your ¼" seam allowance
is accurate—all blocks assume an
accurate ¼" seam._

MAKING STAR BLOCKS

_Each Star block uses a different
blue-violet and yellow-orange fabric
combination. From 1 blue-violet
fabric, use a 4½" × 4½" square and
8 matching 2½" × 2½" squares.
From 1 yellow-orange fabric, use
4 rectangles 2½" × 4½" and
4 matching 2½" × 2½" squares for
each block._

1. Place 1 blue-violet 2½" × 2½"
square to an edge of 1 yellow-orange
2½" × 4½" rectangle, right sides
together. Sew on the diagonal line.
Press. Square up the edge of the
flipped blue-violet fabric so that it
matches the edge of the yellow-orange
rectangle, if necessary, and then trim
out the back 2 layers of fabric.

Draw a   Stitch on   Press and
diagonal   line.   trim.
line.

2. Place another blue-
violet 2½" × 2½" square
to the opposite edge of
the same yellow-orange
rectangle, right sides
together. Press. Square up the edge,
and trim the back 2 layers of fabric.
This unit becomes 2 of the Star's
points.

Press and
trim.

3. Repeat Steps 1 and 2 to sew the
remaining 3 rectangles and 6 squares
to make additional Star point units.

4. Sew 2 yellow-orange 2½" squares
to opposite ends of Star point unit.
Press toward the squares. Make 2.

5. Sew Star point units to opposite
sides of 1 blue-violet 4½" square.
Press toward the square.

6. Arrange and sew the rows together.
Press.

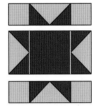 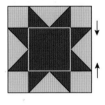

7. Repeat Steps 1–6 to sew additional
yellow-orange and blue-violet fabrics
to make a total of 13 Star blocks.

MAKING CIRCLE BLOCKS

_There are many triangles in this quilt,
and they could be made with half-
square triangle blocks. However, in
this quilt, I gave this idea a little twist—
although there are triangles, they are
made using squares and rectangles._

1. Using 4 blue-violet 2½" × 4½"
rectangles, and 8 yellow-orange
2½" squares, make 4 units as shown.
Draw diagonal lines on the wrong side
of the squares. Sew on drawn lines.

Press and square up the edges, and trim back 2 layers of fabric.

Stitch on line.   Press and trim.

2. Repeat Step 1 using 4 more blue-violet 2½″ × 4½″ rectangles and 8 yellow-orange 2½″ squares to make 4 units as shown.

Stitch on line.   Press and trim.

3. Using 4 blue-violet 2½″ × 6½″ rectangles and 8 yellow-orange 2½″ squares, make 4 units as shown.

Stitch on line.   Press and trim.

4. Using 4 more blue-violet 2½″ × 6½″ rectangles and 8 yellow-orange 2½″ squares, make 4 units as shown.

Stitch on line.   Press and trim.

5. Arrange and sew together the Star block, 4½″ units, 6½″ units, and 8 yellow-orange 2½″ squares as shown. Make 1 circle block.

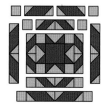

6. Repeat Steps 1–5 using 96 blue-violet 2½″ × 4½″ rectangles, 96 blue-violet 2½″ × 6½″ rectangles, and 480 yellow-orange 2½″ squares to make a total of 13 circle blocks. Block measures 16½″ × 16½″.

Make 13.

MAKING FOUR-PATCH BLOCKS

You will make the Four-Patch blocks using leftover yellow-orange and blue-violet 2½″ strips.

As with the half-square triangle blocks, I added a little twist in this quilt to the Four-Patches. I placed the leftover yellow-orange strips right-side up (they are longer), and then put the blue-violet strips on top, right sides together. I added blue-violet strips, leaving a small space in between, and continued adding until I sewed the length of the yellow-orange strips. Not all yellow-orange strips were long, but I continued to make pairs of yellow-orange and blue-violet strips until I ran out of either color. I did not cut additional strips.

Sew strips together.

Sew strips together.

1. Press all strip sections toward the blue-violet fabrics. Cut into 2½″ sections.

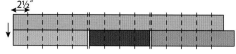

Cut into segments.

2. Arrange 2 segments as shown, and sew together. Press. Make 36 Four-Patch blocks.

Stitch.   Make 36.

ASSEMBLING THE QUILT TOP

1. Arrange the circle blocks, Four-Patch blocks, and 4½" squares as shown. Quilt will be sewn together in 5 horizontal rows.

2. Sew together 3 circle blocks, 12 blue-violet squares, and 60 yellow squares to make a horizontal row. Make 2 each of Row 1 (top) and Row 5 (bottom). Press seams as desired.

3. Sew together 2 circle blocks, 10 Four-Patch blocks, and 38 yellow-orange squares too make Rows 2 and 4. Press.

4. Sew together 3 circle blocks, 16 Four-Patch blocks, and 16 yellow-orange squares to make Row 3. Press.

5. Sew rows together. Press seams as desired.

6. Layer the top with batting and backing. Quilt and bind as desired.

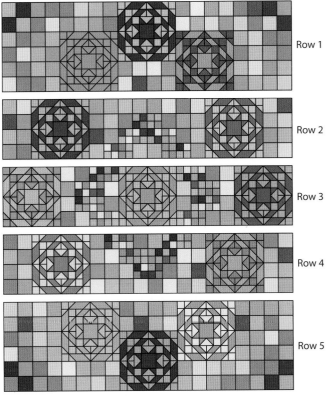

Row 1

Row 2

Row 3

Row 4

Row 5

Quilt assembly

SANDY BONSIB is a teacher by profession and a quilter by passion. She has had quilts published in numerous magazines, has authored several books, and has appeared on the television shows *Simply Quilts* and *Lap Quilting*. She teaches and lectures around the world. Sandy lives in Issaquah, Washington.

WEBSITE: sandybonsib.com

This project originally appeared in *Patchwork Party* by Sandy Bonsib, available from C&T Publishing.

Triple Star

Elena Roscoe

FINISHED QUILT: 66" × 84"

FINISHED BLOCK: 16" × 16"
(unfinished block: 16½" × 16½")

Fabric: Assorted scraps and Flea Market Fancy by Denyse Schmidt, FreeSpirit Fabrics

Block-in-block construction is not as tricky as it looks, even with the smallest of shapes nestled inside larger ones. Elena's Triple Star block is a variation of the traditional Rising Star, but with one extra layer. Each scrappy block features two complementary colors, and the finished stars are sashed in white to allow the eye to hone in on the colorful, vibrant prints in each one. Use this pattern to make Triple Star pillows or piece a quilt that's totally custom, made from stars of different sizes.

Made by Elena Roscoe;
quilted by Angela Walters

Materials

PRINTS: 2¼ yards total, using a variety of scraps, charm squares, or fat quarters for blocks

WHITE: 5 yards for blocks, sashing, and borders

PINK PRINT: ⅞ yard for border

BINDING: ¾ yard

BACKING: 5¼ yards

BATTING: 74" × 92"

Cutting

For a color pairing like the one in Elena's quilt, choose 2 specific colors for each quilter's block kit and pick a variety of prints in each color. WOF = width of fabric.

PRINTS

For fussy-cut centers, cut 12 squares 2½" × 2½". (Also see Fussy Cutting, page 22.)

Cut 48 squares 2½" × 2½".

Cut 48 squares 3½" × 3½".

Cut 48 squares 5½" × 5½".

WHITE

Cut 48 squares 1½" × 1½".

Cut 96 squares 2½" × 2½".

Cut 48 squares 3½" × 3½".

Cut 48 squares 4½" × 4½".

Cut 48 squares 5½" × 5½".

For sashing and borders, cut 22 strips 2½" × WOF, joining as needed to piece longer strips. From these strips, subcut the following pieces:

  8 strips 2½" × 16½" for sashing between blocks

  3 strips 2½" × 52½" for sashing between rows

  2 strips 2½" × 56½" for top and bottom inner borders

  2 strips 2½" × 70½" for side inner borders

  2 strips 2½" × 80½" for side outer borders

  2 strips 2½" × 66½" for top and bottom outer borders

PINK PRINT

Cut 7 strips 3½" × WOF. Join and trim to make 2 strips 3½" × 62½" for top and bottom borders and 2 strips 3½" × 74½" for side borders.

BINDING

Cut 8 strips 2½" × WOF.

Construction

BLOCK ASSEMBLY

1. To make the half-square triangle units, place a white square 2½" × 2½" on top of a print square 2½" × 2½" with right sides together. With a ruler and pencil or Hera marker, mark a diagonal line across the top square.

2. Sew ¼" from the marked line on both sides.

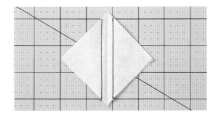

3. Cut on the marked line.

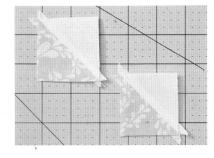

4. Press the seams open. Trim to 1½" × 1½", using a clear ruler with a 45° mark to line up with the diagonal seam. Repeat with 3 additional pairs of 2½" print and white squares.

5. Arrange the inner star with the fussy-cut print in the center. Arrange the half-square triangles so a unit of each color is on each side of the square. Place the 1½" white squares in the corners.

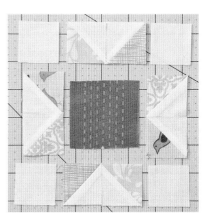

6. Sew together each pair of half-square triangles with right sides facing. Press seams open. Stitch the left and right star points to the center. Stitch the solid corners to the loose star points, and then attach to the top and bottom of the block. This completed star now becomes the center block for the next star.

7. Pair the 3½" print and white squares together. Mark a diagonal line, sew, and cut as described above. Trim to 2½" × 2½".

8. Pair the 5½" print and white squares together. Mark a diagonal line, sew, and cut as described above. Trim to 4½" × 4½".

9. Arrange and sew the pieces together, treating each completed star as the new center.

tip **Fussy Cutting:** The center of each Triple Star block features a sewing notion, such as scissors or thread. Elena used the technique of *fussy cutting*, which is centering a specific print inside of a specific cut of fabric. You'll need a clear ruler or a template and a rotary cutter for fussy cutting. Remember that the fussy-cut square will lose ¼" on each side during block construction, so choose a print that will not be cut off around the edges.

QUILT ASSEMBLY

Refer to the quilt photo (page 20) and to the quilt assembly diagram (below left).

1. Arrange 12 blocks into 4 rows of 3 blocks each. Add the 2½" × 16½" sashing pieces between the blocks in each row. Press.

2. Sew the rows of blocks to the 2½" × 52½" sashing pieces. Press.

3. Add inner white side borders. Press. Add inner white top and bottom borders. Press.

4. Add pink side borders. Press. Add pink top and bottom borders. Press.

5. Add outer white side borders. Press. Add outer white top and bottom borders. Press.

6. Layer, quilt, and bind the quilt.

ELENA ROSCOE has been hooked on the creative process since she began sewing as a little girl. She is active in the
Photo by Jemma Coleman online sewing community, including blogging at *Hot Pink Stitches*, and enjoys interacting with stitch friends from around the globe. Elena lives in South Florida.

WEBSITE: hotpinkstitches.com

This project originally appeared in *Modern Bee—13 Quilts to Make with Friends* by Lindsay Conner, available from Stash Books.

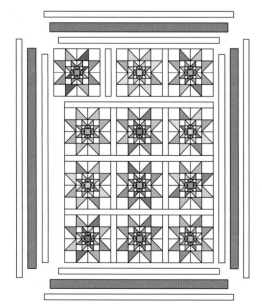

Quilt assembly

Color Stripes

Jan Krentz

This traditional Starburst or Sunburst design is a modern version of a one-patch quilt design. Cut a variety of fabrics into 3˝ or 6½˝ diamonds and arrange them on a design wall. The larger diamonds will create a large quilt very quickly! The biggest challenge will be deciding when the quilt is done and you are ready to trim the edges.

Fabric choices will greatly nfluence the appearance of your quilt. Include some fussy-cut units intermingled with batik fabrics, or create string-pieced strip sets and cut them into diamonds.

Made by Jan Krentz with R. Lynne Lichtenstern; quilted by Debra Geissler; designs by Deb Geissler Enterprises, Inc.

Materials and Cutting

Use the chart (at right) and the quilt diagrams (page 25), to decide which size quilt you wish to make: small, medium, or large. Collect fabrics from your stash and cut diamonds, using the 6½″ diamond pattern (pages 38 and 39) or the 3″ diamond pattern (page 39) in multiples of 8 to create a symmetrical design. Eight diamonds create the center star, and each successive round will have 8 additional diamonds (16, 24, 32, and so on). If you prefer an asymmetrical color placement in your quilt, you might want to photocopy the asymmetrical diagram (page 25) and color in the diamonds to estimate the numbers to cut of various fabrics. The yardage estimates are a guideline only. This is a good quilt to use fabrics from your stash.

Before cutting, press your fabrics; then cut up to 4 layers at once using a sharp new 45 mm or 60 mm rotary cutter. Save any partial fabric pieces remaining at the edges; you may be able to use them at the edges of the quilt top.

Quilt size*	Yardage	Number of diamonds to cut	Diamond ruler size
25″ × 25″ (Outline A)	1 to 3+ yards total	84–100	3″
60″ × 60″ (Outline A)	5 to 8+ yards total	84–100	6½″
35″ × 35″ (Outline B)	2 to 4+ yards total	160–200	3″
84″ × 84″ (Outline B)	9 to 13+ yards total	160–200	6½″
46″ × 46″ (Outline C)	3 to 6+ yards total	276–300	3″
110″ × 110″ (Outline C)	14 to 20+ yards total	276–300	6½″

Small, medium, or large piece of flannel, flannel sheet, flannel-backed tablecloth, or batting for designing the quilt.

Backing and batting: add 6″ to 8″ to the quilt size.

Binding yardages: ³/8 yard, ⁵/8 yard, ½ yard, ⁷/8 yard, ½ yard, 1 yard (in chart order)

* See the quilt diagrams (page 25) for outlines of the various sizes.

Construction

A design wall will make it much easier when laying out the diamonds for this quilt.

1. Determine whether your quilt design will be centered (as in the quilt shown), or if the star will be off-center. Using your flannel, press folds as described below to create a guide for arranging the diamonds. As an alternative, you might mark your existing design wall with tape to create a guide.

For a symmetrical, centered design: Fold the flannel in half lengthwise and crosswise. Press the folds to make prominent creases. Fold the flannel diagonally in both directions and press the folds. The flannel will be divided equally into 8 sections with all folds intersecting in the middle.

For an off-center or asymmetrical design: Evenly fold a section (approximately ⅓) of the flannel lengthwise, creating a strip parallel to the edge. Press the fold. Rotate the flannel, and fold a strip (approximately ⅓) of the flannel widthwise. Press the fold. Fold the flannel diagonally, matching the first creases. Press the diagonal creases.

2. Mount the flannel on a wall, a large piece of cardboard, or a large sheet of foam insulation board.

3. Arrange the diamonds, beginning in the center. Align diamonds in the sections, using the creases to keep the 8 sections orderly. Fill in the edges of the diamond rows with the scraps left over during the cutting process.

4. Assemble the diagonal rows of diamonds, pressing seams open. Use spray starch to stabilize the rows and prevent stretching or distortion.

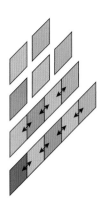

5. Assemble the rows, creating 8 sections. Sew pairs of sections, creating 4 quarter sections. Press the seam open between units.

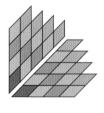

6. Assemble the quarter units into halves; finally join the 2 halves, aligning the center intersection. Pin the intersections along the entire length of the seam and sew the quilt top. The outer edges will be very irregular and ragged at this stage.

7. Press the quilt top neatly; lay the quilt top face down on a large cutting mat. Fold the quilt in half and align the longest straight ruler perpendicular with the fold. Trim the double layers at both ends that are stacked together. Unfold and repeat by folding in the opposite direction and trimming the remaining 2 edges.

Note: If your trimmed quilt top is smaller than you desire, design and add borders to coordinate with the quilt.

8. Layer and baste the quilt top with batting and backing. Quilt as desired and bind.

JAN KRENTZ is an award-winning, internationally-recognized quilt instructor and designer. Jan's motivating presentations and workshops are packed with practical tips, techniques, and methods to ensure success. She is the author of several C&T books, a DVD, and the fast2cut rulers. Jan lives in Poway, California.

WEBSITE: jankrentz.com

This project originally appeared in *Quick Star Quilts & Beyond* by Jan P. Krentz, available from C&T Publishing.

Color Stripes: Symmetrical quilt diagram in 3 sizes

Color Stripes: Asymmetrical quilt diagram in 3 sizes

Hometown Summer Runner

Sherri McConnell

FINISHED RUNNER: 20" × 46"

FINISHED BLOCK: 12" × 12"

Another favorite star block of mine creates a homey summertime runner perfect for decorating all season long. These stars would also be a lot of fun pieced together from the latest florals and other new arrivals at your local quilt shop.

Pieced by Sherri McConnell; quilted by Gail Begay • *Fabric collection: American Banner Rose by Minick & Simpson for Moda*

Materials

ASSORTED MEDIUM AND DARK PRINTS:
6 fat eighths or 6 squares 10″ × 10″

BLOCK BACKGROUND:* ³⁄₈ yard or 3 fat eighths

SASHING AND INNER BORDER: ¼ yard

OUTER BORDER: ½ yard

BACKING: 1½ yards

BINDING: ³⁄₈ yard

BATTING: 26″ × 52″

* You can use one background fabric (³⁄₈ yard) or a different one for each block (3 fat eighths).

Cutting

ASSORTED PRINT FABRICS (6): Cut 4 squares 4″ × 4″ *from each* for star blocks.

BACKGROUND FABRIC: Cut 4 squares 4″ × 4″ and 4 squares 3½″ × 3½″ for each block (12 squares total of each size).

SASHING AND INNER BORDER FABRIC
Cut 4 strips 1½″ × 12½″.

Cut 2 strips 1½″ × 40½″.

OUTER BORDER FABRIC
Cut 2 strips 3½″ × 14½″.

Cut 3 strips 3½″ × width of fabric.

BINDING FABRIC: Cut 4 strips 2¼″ × width of fabric.

SHERRI MCCONNELL, inspired by a rich family heritage of women who love sewing, began to sew at age 10. In the early 1990s, encouraged and taught by her grandmother, she began her quilting journey. Through blogging and creating, she has come to love designing and sharing her quilting. She lives in rural southern Nevada.

WEBSITE: aquiltinglife.com

This project originally appeared in *A Quilting Life* by Sherri McConnell, available from C&T Publishing.

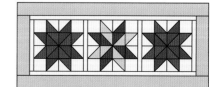

Construction

BLOCK ASSEMBLY

Seam allowances are ¼″ unless otherwise noted.

1. Pair up the 6 print fabrics, choosing 2 fabrics for each of the 3 star blocks.

2. Using 2 squares from each of the 2 fabrics for a single block, make 4 half-square triangles. Trim to 3½″ square.

Make 4.

tip I have found that by pressing seams open on half-square triangle units, the finished units are more accurate.

3. Using 4 matching background squares and the remaining medium/dark print fabric squares, make 8 half-square triangles, 4 of each fabric.

Make 4 of each.

4. Arrange the 12 half-square triangles and the 4 matching

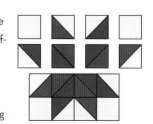

Block assembly

3½″ × 3½″ background squares as shown. Sew the units together in rows. Press.

5. Repeat Steps 1–4 to make 3 blocks. Note in the quilt photo (page 25) that red is in the opposite position in one of the blocks.

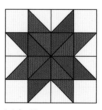

Make 3.

RUNNER ASSEMBLY

1. Arrange and sew the 3 blocks together with the 1½″ × 12½″ sashing strips, beginning and ending with a sashing strip. Press the seams toward the sashing.

2. Sew the 1½″ × 40½″ strips to the long edges of the runner. Press toward the strips.

3. Sew the 3½″ × 14½″ outer border strips to the short ends of the runner. Press the seams toward the outer borders.

4. Sew the 3½″ × 40″ outer border strips together to make a long strip. Cut 2 strips 46½″ long. Sew the strips to the long edges of the runner. Press the seams toward the outer borders.

5. Layer the backing, batting, and runner top. Quilt as desired. Bind the edges.

Runner assembly

Delightful Diamond Chain

Barbara H. Cline

The classic diamond chain pattern was used to create this dramatic quilt. The graduation in the colors of the background fabrics gives the quilt depth, and the diamond chain running from corner to corner through each block makes it look challenging. The method used to make the diamond chain includes strip piecing.

Made by Barbara Cline; machine quilted by Patricia Bird

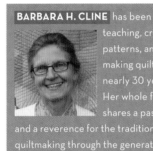

BARBARA H. CLINE has been teaching, creating patterns, and making quilts for nearly 30 years. Her whole family shares a passion and a reverence for the tradition of quiltmaking through the generations. Barbara lives in Shenandoah Valley, Virginia.

WEBSITE: delightfulpiecing.com

This project originally appeared in *Star Struck Quilts* by Barbara H. Cline, available from C&T Publishing.

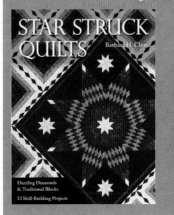

Materials

All yardage is based on 42″-wide fabric. (The numbers in parentheses are for making a smaller 79½″ × 102″ quilt.)

Center Star

When choosing the fabrics for the center star, use tone-on-tone prints, marbled fabrics, or solids rather than multicolored prints that will distract your eye from the pattern as a whole.

Center star

WHITE: ⅜ yard

LIGHTEST RED: ⅜ yard for star

LIGHT RED: ½ yard for star

MEDIUM RED: ⅝ yard for star

DARK RED: ¾ yard for star

LIGHT GRAY: ⅞ yard

BLACK: 2¼ yards for background and second border

RED: ⅓ yard for first border

BINDING: ½ yard

BACKING: 3⅛ yards

BATTING: 56″ × 56″

TEMPLATE PLASTIC

(continued on page 28)

Background Blocks and Borders

RED SOLID: ½ (⅓) yard for eight-pointed star

RED PRINT 1: ½ (⅓) yard for eight-pointed star

RED PRINT 2: 1⅛ (¾) yards for diamonds running through quilt

Background block

BLACK: 1½ (1⅓) yards for background behind eight-pointed star and first border

DARK GRAY: 1¼ (¾) yards for second background

MEDIUM-DARK GRAY: 1½ (⅞) yards for third background

MEDIUM GRAY: 2 (1⅛) yards for fourth background

MEDIUM-LIGHT GRAY: 2¾ (1⅝) yards for fifth background

LIGHT GRAY: 3⅜ (2¼) yards for background behind diamond chain

RED/BLACK PRINT: 1⅔ (1½) yards for second border

BACKING: 8⅔ (7¼) yards

BINDING: ⅞ (¾) yard

BATTING: 104″ × 115″ (87″ × 110″)

TEMPLATE PLASTIC

Cutting

Photocopy patterns (pages 37 and 38) at 200% and use as indicated. Label all the pieces. WOF = width of fabric. (The numbers in parentheses are for making a smaller 79½″ × 102″ quilt.)

CENTER STAR

White:

Cut A—2 strips 1¾″ × WOF.

Cut I—2 strips 1¾″ × WOF; subcut 1¾″ diamonds for a total of 16.

Lightest red star:

Cut B—4 strips 1¾″ × WOF.

Light red star:

Cut C—6 strips 1¾″ × WOF.

Medium red star:

Cut D—8 strips 1¾″ × WOF.

Dark red star:

Cut E—10 strips 1¾″ × WOF.

Light gray:

Cut F—12 strips 1¾″ ×WOF.

Cut H—2 strips 1¾″ × WOF; subcut 1¾″ diamonds for a total of 16.

Black:

Cut G—7 strips 1¾″ × WOF.

Cut J—1 strip 2¼″ × WOF; subcut 16 squares 2¼″ × 2¼″.

Cut K—1 strip 3¾″ × WOF; subcut 4 squares 3¾″ × 3¾″, and cut diagonally twice for a total of 16 triangles.

Cut L—6 strips 3⅝″ × WOF; subcut 16 pieces, using center star pattern.

Cut side triangles—1 square 18¾″ × 18¾″; subcut diagonally twice for a total of 4 triangles.

Cut 6 strips 2¾″ × WOF.

Red border:

Cut 6 strips 1¼″ × WOF.

Binding:

Cut 6 strips 2¼″ × WOF.

BACKGROUND BLOCKS AND BORDERS

Red solid:

Cut A2—7 (4) strips 1⅝″ × WOF; subcut 1⅝″ diamonds for a total of 108 (60).

Red print 1:

Cut A1—7 (4) strips 1⅝″ × WOF; subcut 1⅝″ diamonds for a total of 108 (60).

Red print 2:

Cut diamond chain—20 (12) strips 1¾″ × WOF.

Black:

Cut B—8 (5) strips 3½″ × WOF; subcut 81 (45) squares 3½″ × 3½″, and cut diagonally twice for a total of 324 (180) triangles.

Cut first border—12 (10) strips 1¾″ (2½″) × WOF.

Dark gray:

Cut C—22 (12) strips 1⅝″ × WOF; subcut pieces with pattern C for a total of 108 (60).

Medium-dark gray:

Cut D—27 (15) strips 1⅝″ × WOF; subcut pieces with pattern D for a total of 108 (60).

Medium gray:

Cut E—36 (20) strips 1⅝″ × WOF; subcut pieces with pattern E for a total of 108 (60).

Medium-light gray:

Cut F—54 (30) strips 1⅝″ × WOF; subcut pieces with pattern F for a total of 108 (60).

Light gray:

Cut G—6 (4) strips 3″ × WOF; subcut pieces 2″ × 3″ for a total of 120 (72).

Cut H—1 (1) strip 3″ × WOF; subcut 4 squares 3″ × 3″, and cut diagonally once for a total of 8 (8) triangles.

Cut diamond chain—40 (24) strips 2″ × WOF.

Red/black print:

Cut second border—8 (8) strips 2¼″ (4½″) × length of fabric.

Binding:

Cut 11 (10) strips 2¼″ × WOF.

Center Star: *Making Large Diamonds*

1. Sew the strips together, offsetting the strips by 1¾". Trim the left edge of the set to make a 45° angle. Cut 16 diamond strips 1¾" wide from strip sets 1, 2, and 3. Cut 8 diamond strips 1¾" wide from strip set 4.

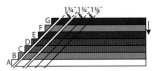

Make 2 of strip set 1. Cut 16.

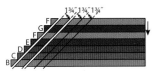

Make 2 of strip set 2. Cut 16.

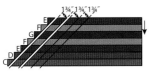

Make 2 of strip set 3. Cut 16.

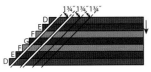

Make 1 of strip set 4. Cut 8.

2. Arrange the diamond strips for the large diamond. Numbers indicate the original strip set numbers. Press. Make 8 large diamonds.

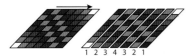

Make 8.

3. Press the diamonds into the proper size and shape. The outside dimensions for the freezer-paper pattern are 9¼" × 9¼". Block each large diamond section.

Center Star: *Making Small Corner Stars*

1. Use pieces H, I, J, and K to lay out 4 small stars for the quilt corners. Make 4 stars.

Make 4.

2. Add an L piece to each side of a small star, mitering each corner. Press the seams toward L. Complete 4 blocks.

Make 4.

Center Star: *Assembling*

1. Referring to the center star layout, sew the top into quarters, and then join the quarters.

Center star layout

2. Add the mitered borders, using the red 1¼" strips and the black 2¾" strips to make the border.

Making Diamond Chains

1. For the diamond chain, sew a red 1¾" strip between light gray 2" strips. Press the seams toward the red. Make 20 (12) strip sets. Then cut 1¾" sections. Use all the strip sets. Cut 300 (180) sections.

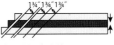

Cut 300 (180).

2. Sew 5 sections from Step 1 together to make a diamond chain, matching and pinning each seam.

Make 60 (36) sections.

3. Sew a light gray G piece to each end of each diamond chain, centering the G piece on the last diamond. Press the seam toward G. Complete 60 (36).

4. Use a see-through ruler and rotary cutter to trim the diamond chains ¼" from the side diamond tips on both sides.

Trim ¼" beyond side diamond tips.

5. Use a see-through square ruler and a rotary cutter to trim off the ends of the diamond chains. Trim at 45° from the end diamond tips.

Trim off fabric at 45° angle ¼" from diamond end tip.

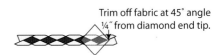

Making Blocks

MAKING SMALL DIAMOND UNITS

Arrange an A1, an A2, and 3 B pieces to form a corner unit for the block. Use Y-seams to sew the unit together. Complete the Y-seam before adding the end B pieces.

Make 108 (60).

COMPLETING THE BLOCKS

1. Sew pieces C, D, E, F, and a small diamond unit together. Make 108 (60). Press the seams away from the small diamond unit.

Make 108 (60).

2. Use a pin to mark the center of the long edge of each unit from Step 1, and match it to the center diamond in the diamond chain unit. Sew a diamond chain between 2 units from Step 1. Make 48 (24). Press the seams away from the diamond chain.

Make 48 (24).

MAKING HALF-BLOCKS

Using the remaining units from Completing the Blocks, Step 1, add a diamond chain to each one. Make 12 (12). Press the seam away from the diamond chain.

Make 12 (12).

Assembling the Quilt Top

1. Arrange 3 blocks and 3 half-blocks with 2 H pieces. The H piece is sewn as part of row 2 and part of row 3. Sew each row together. Press the seams open. Join the rows to make the triangle unit. Make 4 (4).

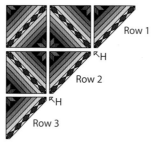

Make 4 (4).

2. After pressing the seams open, the H piece will extend beyond the fabric edges. Trim the edges even with each triangle unit.

3. Trim the star quilt center to 47″ × 47″.

4. Arrange the triangle units around the star center. Because the star center has the diamond border added with the half-blocks, each side of the center has a Y-seam with the triangle units and the center. Sew the triangle units to the center.

5. Referring to the quilt layout for the 96″ × 107¼″ quilt, arrange the blocks around the center from Step 4. (If you are making the smaller 79½″ × 102″ quilt, you will not add the second row to the bottom of the quilt, and you will not add the side rows of blocks.) Arrange the blocks for the additional rows. Check the color placement throughout the quilt.

6. Sew the additional blocks into the number of rows indicated for your quilt size. Press the seams open. Sew the additional rows to the quilt.

7. Add mitered borders, using the black 1¾″ (2½″) strips as the first border and the red/black print 2¼″ (4½″) strips as the outer border.

8. Use your favorite methods to layer, quilt, and bind the quilt with the 2¼″ strips.

Quilt layout, 96″ × 107¼″

Bursting Forth

Barbara H. Cline

FINISHED QUILT: 58″ × 50″

This project features overlays. Placing an overlay of organdy or netting over a fabric produces another value of that fabric's color. Here, overlays create depth in the stars and make them seem to jump out of the quilt. This hexagonal quilt design, with its central star and the interesting shape, would make a dramatic wallhanging.

Made and machine quilted by Barbara H. Cline

BARBARA H. CLINE has been teaching, creating patterns, and making quilts for nearly 30 years. Her whole family shares a passion and a reverence for the tradition of quiltmaking through the generations. Barbara lives in Shenandoah Valley, Virginia.

WEBSITE: delightfulpiecing.com

This project originally appeared in *Simply Triangles* by Barbara H. Cline, available from C&T Publishing.

Materials

Yardage is based on 42″-wide fabric.

Stars

LIGHT GREEN: ⅛ yard

MEDIUM-LIGHT GREEN: ¼ yard

MEDIUM GREEN: ½ yard

DARK GREEN: ⅜ yard

LIGHT BLUE: ⅛ yard

MEDIUM-LIGHT BLUE: ⅜ yard

MEDIUM BLUE: ½ yard

DARK BLUE: ⅝ yard

LIGHT RED: ¾ yard

MEDIUM-LIGHT RED: ⅝ yard

MEDIUM RED: ¾ yard

Other

PRINT FABRIC: 1⅝ yards for border and binding

BACKING FABRIC: 3⅛ yards

BATTING: 64″ × 56″

BLACK NYLON NETTING: 108″ wide, ¾ yard for overlays

TEMPLATE PLASTIC

Cutting

Make templates, using patterns A–G (pages 39 and 40) at 100%. Cut all pattern shapes with the fabric right side up. WOF = width of fabric.

PRINT FABRIC

Cut 5 strips 1⅞″ × WOF.

Cut 6 strips 3½″ × WOF.

Cut 6 strips 2¼″ × WOF.

LIGHT GREEN

Cut 1 strip 2″ × WOF; subcut into 9 diamonds, using template A.

MEDIUM-LIGHT GREEN

Cut 1 strip 1¾″ × WOF; subcut into 9 pieces, using template B.

Cut 1 strip 1¾″ × WOF; subcut into 9 pieces, using template Br.

MEDIUM GREEN

Cut 2 strips 1⅞" × WOF; subcut into 18 pieces, using template C.

Cut 1 strip 2⅛" × WOF; subcut into 9 pieces, using template D.

Cut 1 strip 2⅛" × WOF; subcut into 9 pieces, using template Dr.

DARK GREEN

Cut 1 strip 1⅞" × WOF; subcut into 18 triangles, using template E.

Cut 2 strips 1⅞" × WOF; subcut into 9 pieces, using template F.

Cut 2 strips 1⅞" × WOF; subcut into 9 pieces, using template Fr.

LIGHT BLUE

Cut 1 strip 2" × WOF; subcut into 15 diamonds, using template A.

MEDIUM-LIGHT BLUE

Cut 2 strips 1¾" × WOF; subcut into 15 pieces, using template B.

Cut 2 strips 1¾" × WOF; subcut into 15 pieces, using template Br.

MEDIUM BLUE

Cut 3 strips 1⅞" × WOF; subcut into 30 pieces, using template C.

Cut 2 strips 2⅛" × WOF; subcut into 15 pieces, using template D.

Cut 2 strips 2⅛" × WOF; subcut into 15 pieces, using template Dr.

DARK BLUE

Cut 1 strip 1⅞" × WOF; subcut into 30 pieces, using template E.

Cut 3 strips 1⅞" × WOF; subcut into 15 pieces, using template F.

Cut 3 strips 1⅞" × WOF; subcut into 15 pieces, using template Fr.

LIGHT RED

Cut 1 strip 2" × WOF; subcut into 6 diamonds, using template A.

Cut 1 strip 1⅞" × WOF; subcut into 12 pieces, using template E.

Cut 1 strip 1⅞" × WOF; subcut into 6 pieces, using template F.

Cut 1 strip 1⅞" × WOF; subcut into 6 pieces, using template Fr.

Cut 5 strips 1⅞" × WOF.

MEDIUM-LIGHT RED

Cut 1 strip 1¾" × WOF; subcut into 6 pieces, using template B.

Cut 1 strip 1¾" × WOF; subcut into 6 pieces, using template Br.

Cut 5 strips 1⅞" × WOF.

MEDIUM RED

Cut 2 strips 1⅞" × WOF; subcut into 12 pieces, using template C.

Cut 1 strip 2⅛" × WOF; subcut into 6 pieces, using template D.

Cut 1 strip 2⅛" × WOF; subcut into 6 pieces, using template Dr.

Cut 5 strips 1⅞" × WOF.

NYLON NETTING

Cut 3 strips 6½" × WOF; subcut into 60 rectangles 4" × 6½".

Making Pieced Triangles

The stars feature 2 different triangle designs—unit A triangles and unit B triangles. Half of each unit has a netting overlay, which gives this project its dimensional effect.

UNIT A TRIANGLES

Unit A green triangle— Make 9.

Unit A blue triangle— Make 15.

Unit A red triangle— Make 6.

1. Lay out the pieces for each triangle unit before you begin sewing.

2. Begin with the green fabrics and sew together pieces B, C, and E. Press the seam toward B.

3. Sew together pieces Br, C, and E. Press the seam toward E.

4. Lay nylon netting over the Br/C/E unit and staystitch around the outer edges. Trim the nylon netting even with outside edges of the pieced unit.

5. Sew diamond A to the left and right units.

6. Follow Steps 1–5 to complete 9 green units A.

7. Follow Steps 1–5 to complete 15 blue units A.

8. Follow Steps 1–5 to complete 6 red units A. Note that in these red units, the E triangles are light red fabric.

Overlay gives dimensional effect.

UNIT B TRIANGLES

Unit B green triangle— Make 9.

Unit B blue triangle— Make 15.

Unit B red triangle— Make 6.

1. Lay out the pieces for each triangle unit before you begin sewing.

2. Begin with the green fabrics and sew D to F and press the seam toward D. Then sew Dr to Fr. Press the seam toward Fr.

3. Lay nylon netting over the Dr/Fr unit and staystitch around the outer edges. Trim the nylon netting even with outside edges of the pieced unit.

4. Sew together the D/F and Dr/Fr units. Press.

5. Follow Steps 1–4 to complete 9 green units B.

6. Follow Steps 1–4 to complete 15 blue units B.

7. Follow Steps 1–4 to complete 6 red units B. Note that in these red units, the F and Fr pieces are light red fabric.

Quilting detail

Making Triangles and Diamonds from Strip Sets

In addition to the pieced template triangles, the stars and hexagonal borders feature triangles and diamonds are cut from strip sets.

MAKING THE STRIP SETS

1. On your cutting mat, arrange the $1\frac{7}{8}$"-wide strips in this order from top to bottom: light red, medium-light red, medium red, and print. Do not offset these strips from row to row.

2. Use scant ¼" seams to sew the strips together and press the seams toward the darker fabric. Repeat to make a total of 5 strip sets.

CUTTING THE DIAMONDS

From 3 of the strip sets you will cut 6 right diamonds and 6 left diamonds.

1. To cut the right diamonds, use your ruler to cut a 60° angle off the left side of the strip set. Place the ruler parallel to the 60° angle and make another cut 6" from the previous cut. Cut a total of 6 right diamonds.

6" right diamonds

2. To cut the left diamonds, use your ruler to cut the strip set at a 60° angle in the opposite direction. Place the ruler parallel to the 60° angle and make another cut 6" from the previous cut. Cut a total of 6 left diamonds.

6" left diamonds

CUTTING THE TRIANGLES

From the remaining 2 strip sets, use template G to cut 10 triangles [6"], rotating the template as you move along the strip. Cut 2 additional triangles [6"] from the remainder of the strip sets used to cut the diamonds.

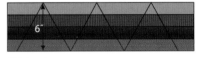

6" triangles

The triangles with the print fabric at the bottom are the ones you will use for this quilt.

....

Assembling the Quilt Top

Refer to the quilt layout diagram to position the units and rows before sewing.

1. To create the center star, place 6 red unit A triangles in a circle with the diamonds in the center, and match 6 red unit B triangles to the red unit A triangles.

2. Add 5 blue unit A triangles around the top red unit B. Repeat on every other red star point. Match a blue unit B triangle to each blue unit A triangle.

3. At the remaining tips of the red star, add 3 green unit A triangles. Match a green unit B triangle to each of the green unit A triangles.

4. Add the left and right diamonds and the strip-pieced triangles as shown in the quilt layout diagram.

5. Sew the triangles and diamonds in diagonal rows as shown. Press the seams open.

6. Sew together the center rows and then add the 2 right rows and the 2 left rows. Press.

7. Attach the borders, using the print 3½″ strips.

8. Use your favorite methods to layer, quilt, and bind with the 2¼″ strips. I decided to quilt a slight wave across the quilt. I echoed that line about 4 times; at the fifth line, halfway across the quilt, I created a new wave heading toward an edge and echoed that line 4 times. I kept repeating this idea over the whole quilt.

Quilt layout

Alternating Stars

Natalia Bonner and Kathleen Whiting

FINISHED QUILT: 75″ × 90″

FINISHED BLOCK: 15″ × 15″

Fabric: Dainty Blossoms by Carina Gardner for Riley Blake Designs

This is a striking quilt that appears to be two different blocks, a Pinwheel and an Eight-Pointed Star. It's really one large block with an eight-pointed star at the center. The block's corners form pinwheels when the blocks are set together. The secret is in the fabric placement! This is a great quilt to show off two of your favorite prints or even two different solid colors and a background color.

Designed, pieced, and quilted by Natalia Bonner and Kathleen Whiting

Materials

Yardage is based on 42"-wide fabric.

Finished size	Baby 45" × 45"	Throw 60" × 60"	Coverlet 75" × 90"
Blue fabric	1¼ yards	1⅞ yards	3¼ yards
Brown fabric	1 yard	1¾ yards	2½ yards
White fabric	1⅛ yards	1¾ yards	3 yards
Backing fabric	3 yards	4 yards	5½ yards
Binding fabric	⅓ yard	½ yard	¾ yard
Batting	53" × 53"	68" × 68"	83" × 98"

Cutting

Cut the squares diagonally once or twice as indicated by the symbols.

Cut		Baby 9 blocks	Throw 16 blocks	Coverlet 30 blocks
Blue fabric	3⅜" × 3⅜" squares	18	32	60
	3⅜" × 3⅜" squares	90 (180 triangles)	160 (320 triangles)	300 (600 triangles)
Brown fabric	6¼" × 6¼" squares	9 (36 triangles)	16 (64 triangles)	30 (120 triangles)
	3⅜" × 3⅜" squares	36	64	120
	3⅜" × 3⅜" squares	18 (36 triangles)	32 (64 triangles)	60 (120 triangles)
White fabric	6¼" × 6¼" squares	9 (36 triangles)	16 (64 triangles)	30 (120 triangles)
	3⅜" × 3⅜" squares	18	32	60
	4" × 4" squares	36	64	120

Construction

SEWING THE BLOCK

To make an Alternating Stars block, follow these steps. Seam allowances are ¼" unless otherwise indicated. Follow the pressing arrows.

1. Use a brown 3⅜" × 3⅜" square and a blue 3⅜" × 3⅜" square to create 2 half-square triangles. Make a total of 4 half-square triangles.

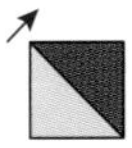

2. Sew the 4 half-square triangles together in pairs, and then sew the pairs together to create a pinwheel.

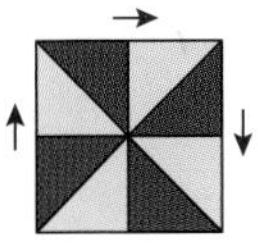

3. Sew a brown 3⅜" triangle and 3 blue 3⅜" triangles to the sides of a 4" × 4" white square. Make 4.

tip For best results, sew opposite sides first and press before sewing the remaining two sides.

4. Sew a brown 3⅜" × 3⅜" square and a white 3⅜" × 3⅜" square together to make 2 half-square triangles. Make a total of 4 half-square triangles.

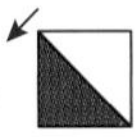

5. Sew a blue 3⅜" triangle to each brown side of the half-square triangle from Step 4. Make 4.

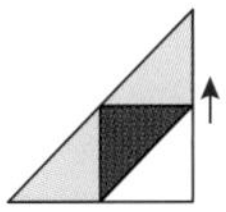

6. Sew a brown 6¼" triangle and a white 6¼" triangle together, matching the short sides. Make 4.

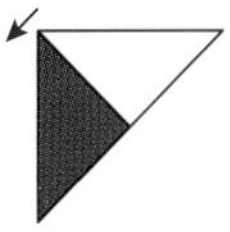

7. Sew the triangle unit from Step 6 to the unit from Step 5. Make 4.

8. Sew 2 units from Step 7 to the unit from Step 3. Note the position of the brown triangle in the center unit. Make 2.

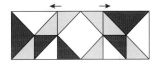

9. Sew a unit from Step 3 onto each side of the pinwheel from Step 2, again noting the position of the brown triangle.

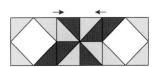

10. Sew the 3 block sections together.

11. Repeat these steps to make the number of blocks needed:

Baby size: 9 blocks

Throw: 16 blocks

Coverlet: 30 blocks

Block assembly

PUTTING IT ALL TOGETHER

Refer to the quilt assembly diagram to find the size quilt you are making. For the baby size, sew 3 rows of 3 blocks. For the throw, sew 4 rows of 4 blocks. For the coverlet, sew 6 rows of 5 blocks. Always press the seams in alternating directions from row to row.

FINISHING

Layer, quilt, and bind the quilt.

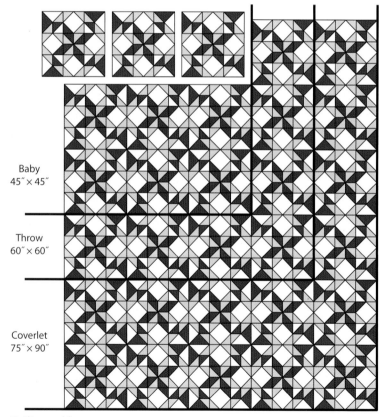

Baby
45″ × 45″

Throw
60″ × 60″

Coverlet
75″ × 90″

Quilt assembly

NATALIA BONNER first learned how to piece and quilt on her home sewing machine, and has been quilting professionally for many years. Natalia is a teacher, pattern designer, and popular blogger with numerous awards for her work. She lives in St. George, Utah.

Photo by Whitnee North

KATHLEEN WHITING has been sewing for decades. In 2010 Kathleen was named the first *McCall's Quilting* Quilt Design Star. She has won numerous awards for her quilts, and her designs have been published in several magazines. She lives in Heber, Utah.

Photo by Whitnee North

WEBSITE: pieceandquilt.com

This project originally appeared in *Modern One-Block Quilts* by Natalia Bonner and Kathleen Whiting, available from C&T Publishing.

Patterns

Delightful Diamond Chain

(page 27)

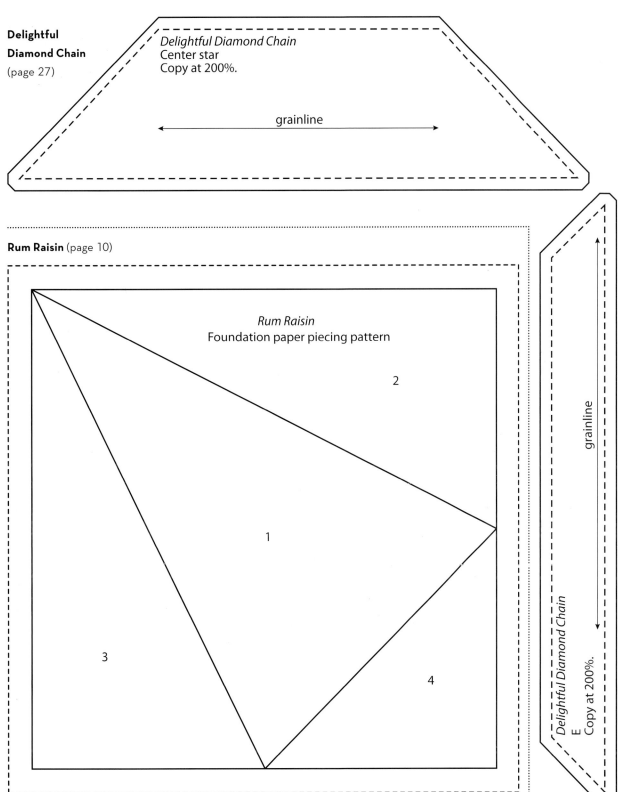

Delightful Diamond Chain
Center star
Copy at 200%.

grainline

Rum Raisin (page 10)

Rum Raisin
Foundation paper piecing pattern

2

1

3

4

grainline

Delightful Diamond Chain
E
Copy at 200%.

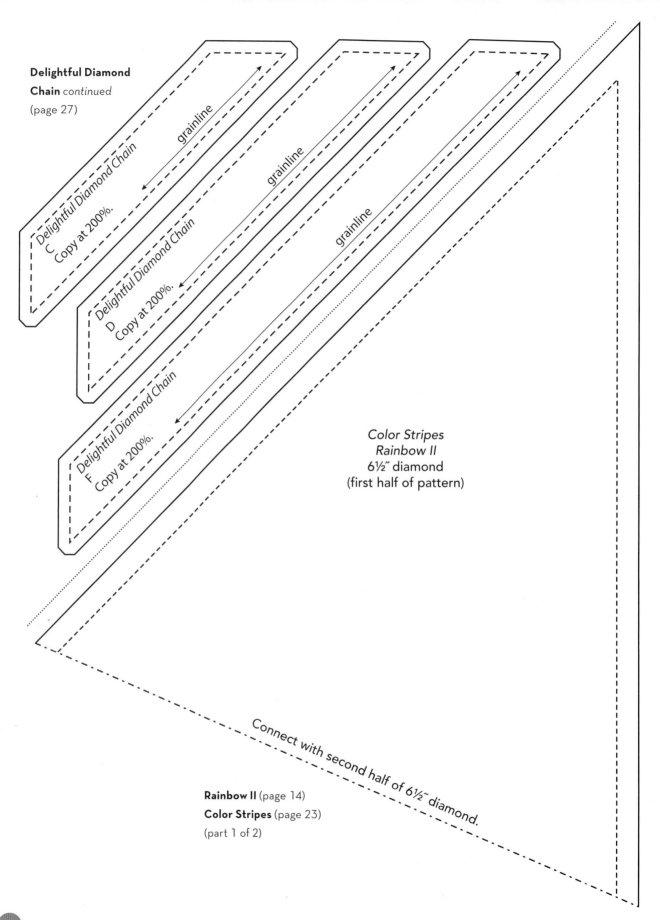

Delightful Diamond

Chain *continued*

(page 27)

Delightful Diamond Chain
C
Copy at 200%.

grainline

Delightful Diamond Chain
D
Copy at 200%.

grainline

Delightful Diamond Chain
F
Copy at 200%.

grainline

Color Stripes
Rainbow II
6½˝ diamond
(first half of pattern)

Connect with second half of 6½˝ diamond.

Rainbow II (page 14)

Color Stripes (page 23)

(part 1 of 2)

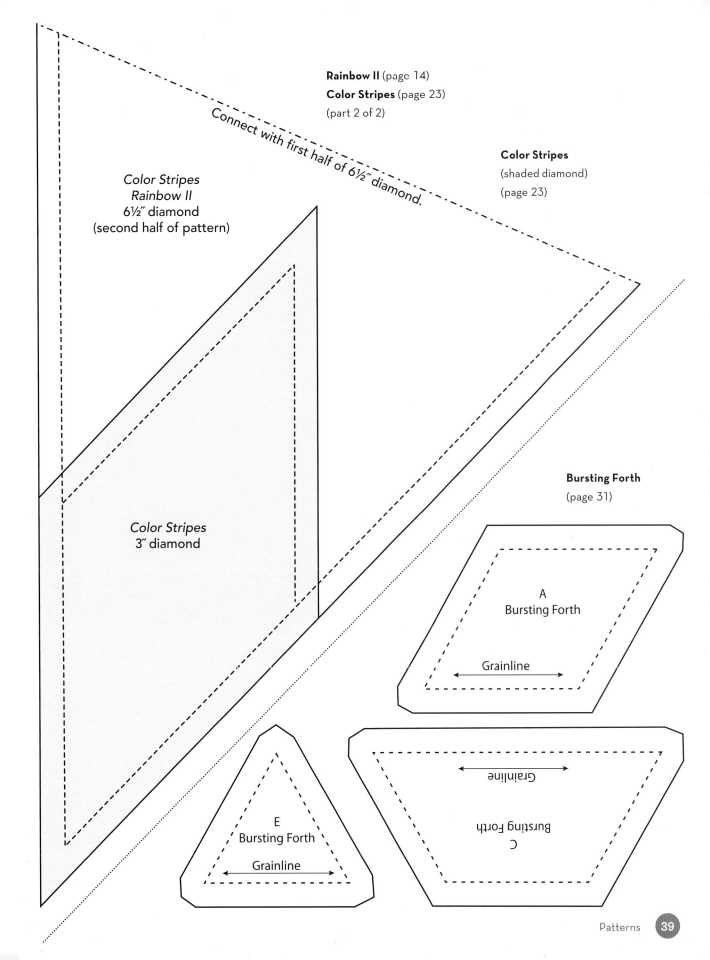

Rainbow II (page 14)
Color Stripes (page 23)
(part 2 of 2)

Color Stripes
(shaded diamond)
(page 23)

Connect with first half of 6½″ diamond.

Color Stripes
Rainbow II
6½″ diamond
(second half of pattern)

Color Stripes
3″ diamond

Bursting Forth
(page 31)

A
Bursting Forth

Grainline

E
Bursting Forth

Grainline

C
Bursting Forth

Grainline

Bursting Forth *continued*
(page 31)

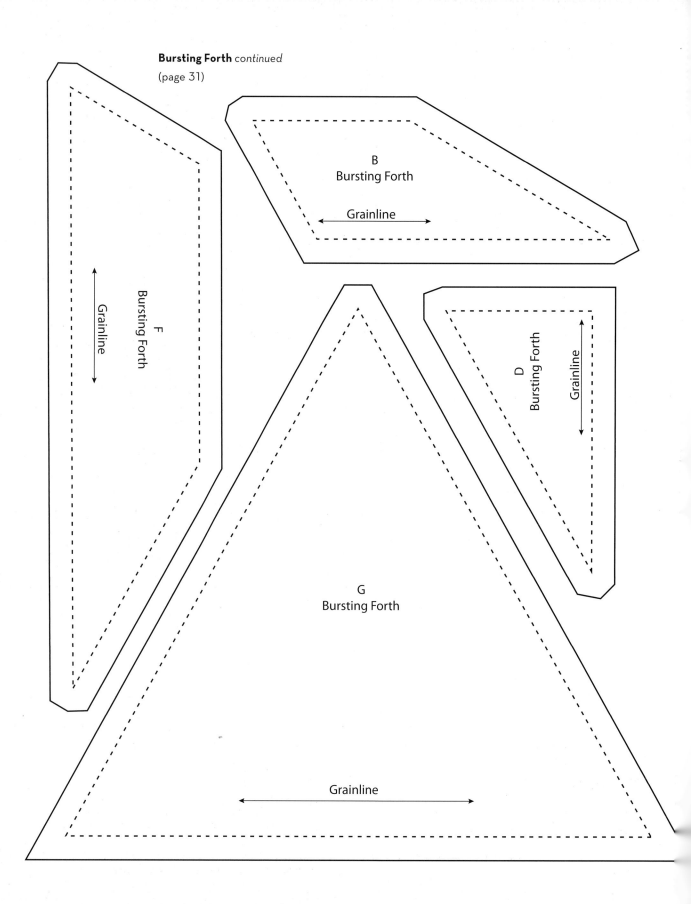

B
Bursting Forth

Grainline

F
Bursting Forth

Grainline

D
Bursting Forth

Grainline

G
Bursting Forth

Grainline